THE ROMAN COOKERY BOOK

a critical translation of

THE ART OF COOKING

by APICIUS

for use in the study and the kitchen

by
BARBARA FLOWER
and
ELISABETH ROSENBAUM

With drawings by
KATERINA WILCZYNSKI

ISBN: 978-1-63923-111-9

Printed: September 2021

Cover Art By: Paul Amid

Published and Distributed By:
Lushena Books
607 Country Club Drive, Unit E
Bensenville, IL 60106
www.lushenabks.com

ISBN: 978-1-63923-111-9

Printed in the United States of America

THE ROMAN COOKERY BOOK

a critical translation of

THE ART OF COOKING

by APICIUS

for use in the study and the kitchen

by

BARBARA FLOWER

and

ELISABETH ROSENBAUM

With drawings by
KATERINA WILCZYNSKI

BRITISH BOOK CENTRE
New York

PREFACE

The idea of this new translation of Apicius was conceived by Barbara Flower at one of her supper parties in the winter of 1952. For both of us it was to be a kind of recreation from our daily work. We began by cooking some of the dishes at random, in order to get the right touch for Roman cooking. When we felt we had acquired a certain skill we became more systematic and more ambitious, and regularly arranged Roman dinner parties to which we invited friends who could judge our interpretations of the recipes. We then proceeded to discuss the recipes one by one, and only after we had gone through the entire book in this manner did we start to write down our translation.

When Barbara Flower died in July 1955 we had worked through the whole book together, and the translation of most of Book I, the whole of Book II, and most of Book III had been written. In the following winter I resumed work alone. Had she lived to see the final result it would certainly contain fewer faults.

The book is meant to be used as a cookery-book rather than read as a curiosity of literature. The introduction is arranged for the convenience of those who are equally at home (as good scholars are apt to be) in the study and the kitchen; those more interested in the practical cookery side might start reading it at page 18.

I wish to thank all those who gave their criticism and advice: Professor P. Maas, who kindly gave me his advice on technical problems in the edition of the Latin text; D. M. Davin, E. Frankfort, and D. P. Walker, who helped to correct the English; J. Liversidge and V. Scholderer, who contributed chapters to the introduction; H. Buchthal and A. M. Meyer, who read part of the proofs; M. Webster and A. Williamson, who typed the manuscript; J. Chadwick, C. Mitchell, and

J. Reynolds, who helped in various ways ; and all the friends who bravely came to our dinner parties.

I hope our new Apicius will serve the purpose we and he intended. May it give those who use it as much delight as it gave us while we worked on it together.

June 1957   ELISABETH ROSENBAUM

NOTE

Thanks are due to the Teubner Verlag, of Leipzig, who have given permission for the use here of the Latin text of Apicius, published by them, and edited by C. Giarratano and F. Vollmer.

CONTENTS

INTRODUCTION

I. THE TEXT AND ITS AUTHOR

Cookery-books seem to have been numerous in antiquity, but only one has come down to us, and that is in Latin. It bears the name of Apicius. It is preserved in two ninth-century manuscripts. One of them was written in Tours during one of the most important periods in the history of the Tours scriptorium, under Abbot Vivian (844–851); the other was probably written in Fulda. The Tours Manuscript, now in the Vatican Library (Urb. lat. 1146), was not made for every-day use; it is distinguished by a decoration which could hardly have withstood the atmosphere of the kitchen: the tables of contents of the first book are framed by arches in a way usually reserved for the Canon Tables of Gospel books.[1] The other manuscript was brought from Fulda to Italy in 1455, came into the Phillips Collection in Cheltenham in the early nineteenth century, and is now in the Library of the Academy of Medicine in New York.[2] Both manuscripts derive from a common archetype which we know to have been in Fulda, and from which Poggio had excerpts made in the early fifteenth century.[3]

Apart from these manuscripts, some excerpts—made by a certain Vinidarius, an Ostrogoth living in North Italy in the fifth or sixth century—have survived in an eighth-century manuscript.

The cookery-book aroused the interest of the Renaissance humanists, and especially that of the physicians among them, who were attracted by its importance for diet. A number of fifteenth-century manuscripts, probably all depending on the Vatican codex, exist in various libraries of Europe, and we can gather from the early printed editions that the educated society of Northern Italy appreciated a text which afforded an insight into the daily life of the Romans.[4]

9

The earliest date connected with the printing of Apicius'
text is recorded in Panzer's *Annales* (Vol. II, p. 64, No.* 350),
where he quotes from an earlier source the note of an edition
signed by Guillermus Le Signerre of Milan "Anno domini.
MCCCCLXXXX. die. viii. mensis Ianuarii," but only to
stigmatize it as "editio spuria," adding "cf. edit. ann. 1498."
Panzer is unquestionably right in his condemnation, the
supposed edition of 1490 being a 'ghost' raised by some mis-
reading of the colophon of the true edition printed "Mediolani
per magistrum Guilermum Signerre Rothomagensem Anno
dñi. Mcccclxxxxviii. die. xx. mensis Ianuarii." The erasure,
deliberate or otherwise, of the two x's after 'die' in a copy of
this would be enough to account for the error. Two issues of
the 1498 edition are known, one in which the title reads
APICIUS DE RE QUOQUINARIA with Le Signerre's device
below and the three following pages devoted to a dedicatory
letter from Antonius Motta to Ioannes Mollus, secretary to the
Duke of Milan, and some verses by Motta and Bernardinus
Mollus, while in the other issue the title reads "Appicius
Culinarius" with the device of the publisher Ioannes de
Legnano, and is followed by a letter of Blasius Lanciloti to
Bartholomæus Merula and a "carmen subitarium" of Ludo-
vicus Vopiscus addressed to Ioannes Antonius Riscius. The
rest of the book is the same in both issues. (For a full descrip-
tion see the *Gesamtkatalog der Wiegendrucke*, No. 2267.)

On November 9, 1497, the Duke of Milan granted a privilege
of copyright for five years to one Ioannes Passiranus de Asula
in respect of six classical texts, one of which was "Apicius de
cibariis." This obviously refers to the present edition, which
was shared between the printer and Legnano, as the title-pages
of the two issues show. Legnano's copies seem to have been
destined for the Venetian market, where customers were likely
to be attracted by the dedication to Bartholomæus Merula,
"preceptor of the children of the magnific Georgius Cornelius"
—*i.e.*, the Venetian patrician Giorgio Cornaro, brother of the
Queen of Cyprus. This issue was reprinted about the turn

of the century at Venice, anonymously and without date (no doubt with a view to avoiding any difficulties which the Milanese privilege might raise), but with the types of Bernardinus (de Vitalibus) Venetus, and having two tracts of Suetonius incongruously subjoined (*Gesamtkatalog*, No. 2268). This edition in turn served as a model for that of Ioannes Tacuinus (Venice, 1503), from which, however, Suetonius is again omitted.

The anonymous Venetian edition has been accepted as the *editio princeps* by the editors of the Teubner Apicius and others, but all the circumstances go to show that this honour belongs to Le Signerre's work of 1498. His issue of it is the only homogeneous printing of the three in question, inasmuch as both the dedication at the beginning and the verses at the end are Milanese, and if the Venetian edition were earlier it would be hard to understand why the preliminaries should point to Venice and yet the addenda to Milan.

The first critical edition of the text by Albanus Torinus was published in Basle in 1541. It gives a kind of translation into humanist Latin, and has many arbitrary conjectures and additions. The next edition, by the physician Gabriel Humelberg (Zürich, 1542), is a masterpiece of classical philology of the time. Humelberg based his text on good manuscripts, among which he names an "antiquum manuscriptum exemplar" now lost. The next editor was the personal physician of Queen Anne of England, Martin Lister. His edition, following Humelberg fairly closely, was published in 1705 in London and in 1709 in Amsterdam. Of the other editions, that of Theophilus Schuch (Heidelberg, 1866 and 1874) deserves mentioning because of its badness. He abolished the division by chapters and paragraphs extant in the manuscripts and numbered the recipes right through. Moreover, he incorporated the excerpts of Vinidarius, inserting them in places where in his opinion they fitted best. Above all, he disfigured the text by numerous baseless conjectures.

The latest and, by our standards, the only reliable edition is that by C. Giarratano and F. Vollmer (Leipzig, Teubner, 1922).

The style of the cookery-book and the name of its author present a number of problems. The admirable study by E. Brandt, the last scholar to investigate these problems, has solved them at least in broad outline, and in such satisfactory manner that we may in general consider his results as facts.[5]

The humanists give the name of the author as Apitius Caelius. Vollmer has shown[6] that the name Caelius is their invention. It seems to originate from a misunderstanding of the corrupt form in which the title of the book is given in the Vatican Manuscript: on the first folio we find API CAE. Vollmer read this Api⟨cii artis magiri- or opsartyti⟩cae ⟨libri X⟩. This leaves us only with the name of Apicius to get on with. Of the various people known by this name, only one is reported to have written books on cooking. This is M. Gavius Apicius, who lived at the time of Tiberius. He is mentioned by several authors. A number of anecdotes are told about him, and his name is linked with several culinary inventions. Seneca is the first to give an account of his death: when, on counting his fortune, he found one day that, after having spent a hundred millions of sesterces mainly on food, he had only ten million sesterces left, and the prospect of starvation before him, he poisoned himself. He wrote, apparently, two cookery-books, one a general recipe book, the other a special book on sauces. His fame hardly diminished with the passage of time; he is mentioned by various Christian authors—for instance, St Jerome; Odo of Cluny speaks of him also. His books must have attained equal fame: Isidorus even states that he was the first to write a cookery-book.

Since Apicius lived in the first century, one would expect his style to be at least as classical as Columella's. The language in our cookery-book, however, is far from classical, or even silver, Latin. It is therefore obvious that what we have before us cannot be Apicius' original book. Brandt has shown that as it has come down to us the cookery-book is the work of an editor who lived in the late fourth or the early fifth century. This person—whose name we do not know, as he published his book under the name of Apicius—made a compilation from various sources. He wanted to combine in one book recipes for the average middle- and lower-class household in town and country with recipes for the more luxurious table. The cookery-book of Apicius offered him only recipes of the latter kind. So he supplemented it from a book on agriculture and domestic science by Apuleius, a book of which fragments have survived in the *Geoponica* and which is probably also reflected in Palladius' book on agriculture; from a Greek book on agriculture; from a dietetic cookery-book, probably also Greek; and from various other sources, chiefly medical writings part of which ultimately go back to Marcellus, a physician who lived under Nero. The popular Latin which permeates the entire book is chiefly due to this editor, although the editions of Apicius and Apuleius which he used may already have contained some popular elements. About three-fifths of the recipes of our book come from Apicius' work. The edition used by our compiler was certainly a fairly late one which already combined Apicius' two books, the general one and the book on sauces—our Books IX and X are almost exclusively recipes for sauces—and which contained also some additions made after Apicius' lifetime. There are, for example, a number of recipes named after emperors or gourmets of repute which had probably slipped into the various Apicius editions made before our compiler set to work. That such different editions of Apicius' book existed is also proved by the excerpts of Vinidarius. He must have used one that contained, apart from Apicius' original recipes, a Greek cookery-book of the Imperial period or at least extracts from such a work.

The arrangement of our book is entirely the work of the fourth- or fifth-century compiler. He seems to have had the titles of the various books before him, although they hardly come from Apicius' original work, and he arranged his material according to these titles. This led him occasionally into difficulties. He took, for instance, recipes out of the context in which he found them because he thought they belonged to some particular book, and then forgot to delete them in their original place, so that several recipes occur twice. The compiler is also responsible for the tables of contents at the beginning of each book. He took as his guide the titles of the recipes. The chapter headings were then inserted into the text from the tables of contents, either by himself or—more likely—by a yet later editor of his compilation. Here too things have occasionally gone wrong. Some headings in the tables of contents are not found in the text, and vice versa.

Comparatively little can be deduced from the compilation about Apicius' original book. It must have contained recipes for a great variety of dishes, and if in our compilation there is only a small number of sweets, this is probably the fault of the compiler. It made use of a great wealth of spices. But the recipes rarely include any indication of quantities, and the ingredients are often simply enumerated without any direction on how they should be used. This means that only experienced cooks could have used Apicius' book. The style is simple and to the point, frequently colloquial, and in general very much like the style of cookery-books down the ages. At one place there is a reference to the illustration of a pan (IV, ii, 14), and we may therefore assume that the book was originally illustrated.

The bulk of our Book I, and most of the short recipes of Book III and the following books, come from the work of Apuleius. Some of these recipes are clearly addressed to the farmer—for example, those which tell how to make bad honey good enough for sale (I, xi, 2), or how to make red wine white (I, v). All the recipes for preserving fruit, meat, and so on, and those on what to do with food in danger of going bad (e.g., I, vi), also come from this source. They often add remarks referring to the result of whatever action is recommended. About half of these recipes have parallels in Palladius and in the *Geoponica*.

The Greek agricultural book is the source for the recipes for spiced wine (I, i, 1–2), Roman vermouth (I, ii), *amulatum* (II, ii, 8), and *apothermum* (II, ii, 10). These recipes are markedly different in style from the rest. Some expressions make sense only in a Greek book: for example, the title "absinthium Romanum" or—in II, ii, 8—"quod Romani colorem vocant." Some of these recipes are different from the majority also in giving precise quantities.

The Greek dietetic cookery-book is represented by such recipes as IV, ii, 4, 5, 8, 9, 29, 31, 36. All these give precise indications of the quantities required. Some of them direct the dishes to be cooked "in thermospodio,"—*i.e.*, hot ashes—and the Latin translation of "thermospodia," "cinis calidus," occurs as well, in one case side by side with the Greek word.

The remaining recipes, taken from various medical writings, are also clearly recognizable. Some have "ad ventrem" in their titles (III, ii, 2–3, 5), others have remarks stating the effect of the dish on the digestive system, and usually they give precise quantities (*e.g.*, I, viii, xviii, xx, 1–2; III, xviii, 2–3). To judge by the style, our compiler probably translated the Greek recipes himself.

II. TRANSLATIONS ; SOME GENERAL REMARKS ON ROMAN COOKING

Apart from the editions mentioned and discussed above, there are a few modern translations: two Italian ones, by G. Baseggio (Venice, 1852), and by P. Buzzi (*Romanorum Scriptorum Corpus Italicum, curante Hectore Romagnoli*, Villasanta, Milan, 1930; re-edited under the title Apicio, *La cucina di Roma*, Veronelli, Milan, 1957); two German translations—R. Gollmer (Breslau–Leipzig, 1909, 2nd ed. Rostock, 1928), and E. Danneil (Leipzig, 1911); a French one, B. Guégan (Paris, 1933); and an English or, rather, American one by J. D. Vehling, *Apicius: Cooking and Dining in Imperial Rome* (Chicago, 1936). We have been unable to see copies of Baseggio's Italian translation or Danneil's German one. Gollmer's, obviously based on Schuch's edition of the text, is arbitrary to the point of becoming a mere paraphrase. Guégan's translation into French has considerable merits. It is made by an expert on gastronomy who is at the same time an historian and well versed in classical literature. Guégan's detailed introduction (with a list of manuscripts and printed editions) and his excellent commentary are so exhaustive that we felt in the present edition we could dispense with a great deal of annotation relating to the species of animals, fish, birds, and vegetables. Wherever we considered it necessary to add notes we are greatly indebted to Guégan's commentary. Any reader who wishes to know more about the nature of the ingredients in our recipes will be well advised to consult this book. Guégan's translation is marred by only one thing: it is based on imperfect editions of the Latin text. Guégan was well aware of the uselessness of Schuch's text, and claims to have based his translation on Humelberg, keeping Schuch's arrangement of the recipes and some of his so-called emendations. But it looks as if he had used rather more of Schuch's edition than the mere arrangement. In any case, it is difficult to understand why he did not use the Teubner edition, which had appeared more than ten years before the publication of his book. In consequence, though he attempts to adhere faithfully to the original, his translation is frequently wrong, in some places so much so that one hardly recognizes the recipe.

Vehling's translation is the only translation into English known to us—it claims to be the first. Vehling was (or is?) a professional cook, and therefore approaches his subject from the practical side. According to the foreword (written by a friend), he acquired his knowledge of Latin at school—which he attended, however, only up to the age of fourteen. It is therefore understandable that his text is so full of mistakes that it becomes almost useless as a translation. But he rightly states in his introduction that the crux of the Apicius question lies in the fact that the scholars who dealt with it before him knew nothing about cooking. Being himself a renowned practitioner of the culinary art, he felt justified in treating his

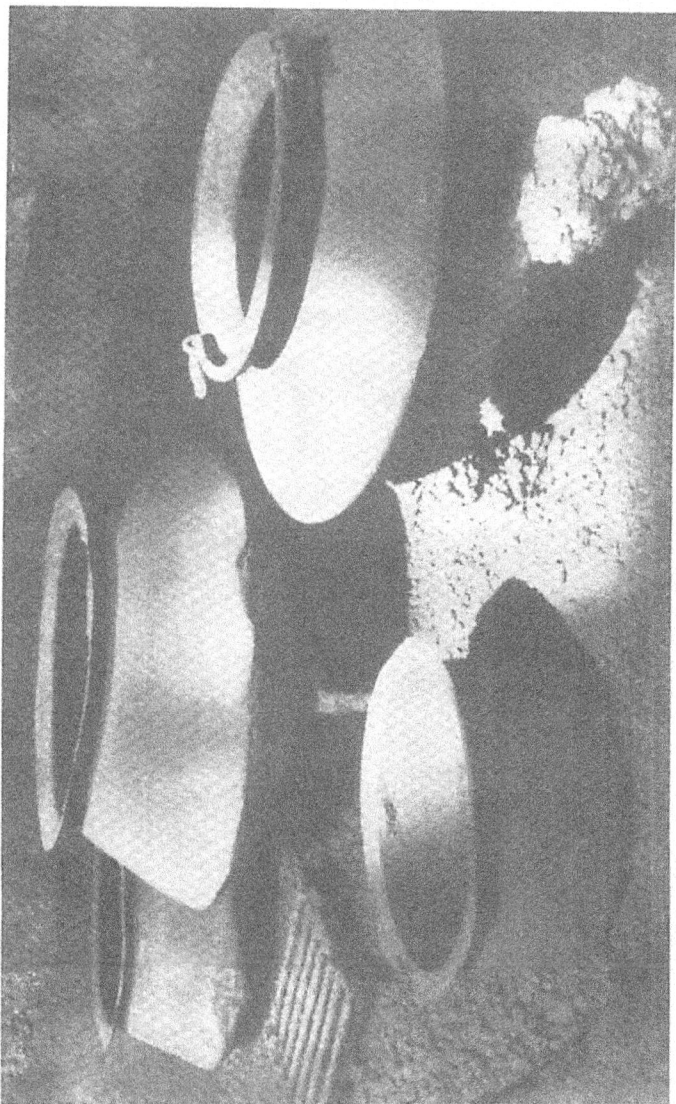

PLATE I

SAUCEPANS ON THE HEARTH IN THE KITCHEN OF THE HOUSE OF THE
VETTII, POMPEII

By courtesy of Istituto Geografico De Agostini-Novara

PLATE II

1   2

3   4

5   6

BRONZE VESSELS IN THE TOWNELEY COLLECTION

(1) (?)*Patella*.   (2) Bowl of type probably used for *bain-marie* cooking.
   (3) (?)*Patina*.   (4) *Caccabus* or small *ahenum*.   (5) Strainer.
                 (6) Frying-pan.

text without too many philological scruples. Unfortunately, he tried his hand at philology as well—he even gives a stemma of all the Apicius editions, manuscripts and printed books alike, including his own translation—and proudly announces that he made use of both the Teubner and the humanist editions— evidently believing these to be independent sources. The result is very curious, and, had he given the Latin, it would look even more grotesque. Whole sentences inserted by the sixteenth-century editor Torinus out of his own imagination appear, along with insertions by other people. Terms which Vehling did not understand are—without much regard to rules of textual criticism—replaced by others which looked more likely to him. This method was bound to lead him astray even on culinary matters. To give an example: disregarding all the literary evidence, he boldly claims that *garum* is a fish sauce of which little is known, whereas *liquamen*[7] simply denotes any kind of liquid, and may therefore be translated as the occasion requires by 'broth' or 'stock' or 'court-bouillon.' His method of translation can be tested by his rendering of recipe V, viii, 2 (B and C), which reads as follows: "*et elixati, sumpto.* Boiled sumptuously. And cook the beans, in a rich manner, remove the seeds and serve (as a salad) with hard eggs, green fennel, pepper, broth, a little reduced wine and a little salt, or serve them in simpler ways, as you may see fit."

The most useful part of Vehling's book is his appendix "Apiciana," which gives a full list with description of all the relevant manuscripts, printed editions, and translations.

Paolo Buzzi's translation, which appears to have escaped the notice of both Guégan and Vehling, became known to us only while the present edition was already in the press so that we could not make full use of it. Qua translation it is probably the best of the existing ones. It prints the Latin text opposite the Italian version; there are a few notes, concerning mainly names of plants and fishes, but there is no commentary. The Latin text is obviously a reprint of the Teubner text (without the apparatus criticus), although this is nowhere stated. In

2—R.C.B.

some cases the translation seems to be based on a text different from that printed in the edition.

Every translation is by its nature partly interpretation. The translation of a cookery-book—and one as concise in places as this—must be interpretation to an even greater extent than other translations. Although we have some experience in cooking, we cannot claim to be professional cooks, and there are some recipes which we understood as little as our predecessors did. We have therefore decided to print the Latin text opposite the English, so that the reader can form his own judgment. We have in general reprinted the text of the Teubner edition, without its apparatus criticus, and we have also omitted the excerpts of Vinidarius printed as an appendix to that edition. We have made a few alterations to the Teubner text; these are partly emendations or restorations of the text of the manuscripts made by Brandt in the book cited on p. 12 or in the footnotes and appendix of the Teubner edition itself; partly they are emendations made by ourselves. Only where our text differs from that of the Teubner edition do we give an apparatus. We have not indicated every instance where we have changed the punctuation of the Teubner edition. We have kept the normalized spelling of the Teubner edition even in cases where our text accepts the corrections of Brandt, who adopted the spelling of the manuscripts. His method is certainly the correct one in a case like Apicius', but as we did not aim at a new text edition we considered the normalized spelling to be more convenient for the reader. In order to enable the reader to compare Guégan's translation, Schuch's recipe numbers are added in italics at the end of each recipe.

Our aim in making this translation was mainly practical. We have tried out many of the recipes, and we found that many could become welcome additions to our menus. In addition, Apicius gives a number of useful hints which could be adopted to vary modern recipes.

The Roman cookery-book was not meant for beginners. The lack of indication of quantities in most recipes makes a basic knowledge of cookery necessary. But we found that with common sense and a little imagination one cannot go wrong on the quantities. We have nevertheless in some cases added the quantities we think correct in a footnote.

Most of the herbs are obtainable in London, at least dried. A number can be obtained from herb-nurseries (seeds or plants). We also found that one may safely omit one or another of the herbs without essentially altering the taste. Recipes for several of the basic ingredients (not given in our book) and some notes on a few of the most important condiments are given in Part III of our introduction, and some explanations and hints will be found with individual recipes and in the Index.

In general we found ourselves in disagreement with the criticism of Roman cooking expressed by a cook on the cook-market in Plautus' Pseudolus (1, 810 ff.)[8]:

> I don't season a dinner the way other cooks do, who serve you up whole pickled meadows in their *patinae*—men who make cows their messmates, who thrust herbs at you, then proceed to season these herbs with other herbs. They put in coriander, fennel, garlic, and horse-parsley, they serve up sorrel, cabbage, beet, and spinach, pouring into this a pound of asafœtida, and pounding up wicked mustard, which makes the pounders' eyes water before they've finished. When they season their dinners they don't use condiments for seasoning, but screech-owls, which eat out the intestines of the guests alive. That is why life is so short for men in this world, since they stuff their bellies with suchlike herbs, fearful to speak of, not just to eat. Men will eat herbs which the cows leave alone.

Nevertheless, the cookery-book shows very clearly that the Romans abhorred the taste of any meat, fish, or vegetable in its pure form. There is hardly a single recipe which does not add a sauce to the main ingredient, a sauce which changes the original taste radically. Some of the more complicated recipes contain so many different things that no single one can be tasted. And at least one of the recipes for a substitute belongs already to the original book of Apicius (IV, ii, 12). With a certain pride, Apicius says at the end of this recipe: no one at table will know what he is eating. Petronius' feast of Trimalchio offers grotesque examples of the Roman passion for the disguise of food, both in appearance and in taste. There is, for instance, the hare done up as Pegasus, which is paralleled in our book in a more humble form in the recipe for 'salt fish without salt fish' (IX, xiii, 1), where a kind of liver paté is shaped into fish. But, then, Mediterranean cooking of to-day shows the very same tendencies. When eating pizza, or bouillabaisse, or Spanish rice, or Spanish omelette, or paella, and a hundred other delicious Southern dishes we may—after having become acquainted with Apicius—feel an additional pleasure to that of the palate—namely, that of gaining practical experience of the survival of antiquity.

A Roman dinner of the more elaborate kind consisted of three main parts: the hors d'œuvre or entrée, called *gustum*, *gustatio*, or *promulsis*; the main course, *mensae primae*; and the dessert course, *mensae secundae*. The *gustatio* was accompanied by *mulsum*.[9] It could consist of eggs prepared in various ways; vegetables raw and cooked, including asparagus, cucumbers, and pumpkins; herbs; lettuce; mushrooms; salt fish; oysters; mussels; snails; also the famous dormice—all these prepared in a variety of ways, so that most of the contents of our Books II–V, VII, and IX–X could be used for the *gustatio*. The *primae mensae* were devoted to roast and boiled meat, poultry, some meat delicacies (which could, however, also be included in the *gustatio*). The recipes in Books VI and VIII, and some in Book VII, would chiefly refer to this course. During this course wine was drunk, usually mixed with water, and in fairly moderate quantities. The *secundae mensae* consisted of fruit or various kinds of sweets. Originally savoury dishes were also served with the third course, and in Trimalchio's feast mussels and snails are included in the *secundae mensae*. But fruit and sweets were the more normal practice in later times. In our cookery-book very little is to be found that could be used for the sweet course—only in Books IV and VII do we find a few recipes suitable for a *secundae mensae*. Sometimes the serious drinking began with the third course, but it usually began after the meal. Apart from the very elaborate feast of Trimalchio, a few simpler Roman menus are recorded. We find, for instance, in Martial's epigrams a few that contain an invitation to a meal. In one he promises his guest a variety of raw herbs, lettuce, eggs, fish, and sow's udder for the *gustatio*, kid, chicken, ham, and sausages for the *primae mensae*, and fruit as dessert. In another it is herbs, lettuce, eggs, cheese, and olives for the *gustatio*, and fish, mussels, sow's udder, and poultry for the *primae mensae*. In Juvenal we find a menu consisting of asparagus and eggs for the *gustatio*, kid and chicken for the *primae mensae*, and fruit for the *secundae mensae*.

III. FISH SAUCES; WINE PREPARATIONS; CHEESE; STARCH; SILPHIUM

In our version we left some of the terms untranslated, as no proper English equivalents exist. These are above all the various basic sauces used for seasoning and the preparations of wine and must used for sweetening and colouring. The first place in importance is taken by the *garum*—or *liquamen*, as it is called in almost all our recipes. This sauce was made in factories, and its use may be compared with that of sauces like Worcester sauce, except for the fact that it was apparently used in lieu of salt. Readers who do not wish to go to the trouble of making their own *liquamen* could therefore use salt instead. One must, however, be aware that without *liquamen* the authentic flavour cannot quite be attained.

Several towns were famous for their *liquamen*—for instance, Pompeii and Lepcis Magna. From Pompeii we know an inscription on a small jar saying: "Best strained liquamen. From the factory of Umbricus Agathopus."[10]

The *Geoponica* give a number of recipes for making *garum*. Chapter 46 of Book XX is entirely devoted to it:

(1–4) The so-called *liquamen* is made as follows: the entrails of fish are thrown into a vessel and salted. Take small fish, either *atherinae*, or small red mullet, or sprats, or anchovy, or any other small fish, and salt all this together and leave to dry in the sun, shaking it frequently. When it has become dry from the heat extract the *garum* from it as follows: take a long fine-meshed basket and place it in the middle of the vessel with the above-mentioned fish, and in this way the so-called *liquamen*, put through the basket, can be taken up. The residue is *allec*.[11]

The Bithynians make it in the following manner: It is best to take large or small sprats, or, failing them, take anchovies, or horse-mackerel, or mackerel, make a mixture of all and put this into a baking-trough. Take two pints of salt to the peck of fish and mix well to have the fish impregnated with the salt. Leave it for one night, then put it in an earthenware vessel which you place open in the sun for 2–3 months, stirring with a stick at intervals, then take it, cover it with a lid and store it away. Some people add old wine, two pints to the pint of fish.

(6) The best *garum*, called *haimation*, is made as follows: take the entrails of tunny fish and its gills, juice, and blood, and add sufficient salt. And leave it in a vessel for two months at the most. Then pierce the vessel and the *garum* called *haimation* will flow out.

These recipes certainly refer to the factory-made *garum*, though a country household, too, could provide the facilities necessary for these lengthy processes. Fortunately, the same chapter of the *Geoponica* contains also a recipe for a quick process:

(5) If you wish to use the *garum* at once—*i.e.*, not expose it to the sun, but boil it—make it in the following manner: Take brine and test its strength by throwing an egg into it to try if it floats; if it sinks the brine does not contain enough salt. Put the fish into the brine in a new earthenware pot, add origan, put it on a good fire until it boils—*i.e.*, until it begins to reduce. Some people also add *defrutum*. Let it cool and strain it two and three times, until it is clear. Seal and store away.

This is the kind of *liquamen* we made and used (we did add the *defrutum*), and the *liquamen* prepared in this way was so good that even considerable quantities could be used without leaving an unpleasant taste.

Liquamen was mixed with water, wine, vinegar, and so on, and was then called *hydrogarum*, *oenogarum*, *oxygarum*, etc. Sometimes other spices were added to the mixture.

A by-product of the *liquamen* manufacture is the so-called *allec*, or *hallec*. It is mentioned in the first *liquamen* recipe as the residue that remains when the *garum* is extracted. Pliny tells us (*Nat. Hist.* XXXI, 8, 44 (95)) that it was also made separately from very small fish that were otherwise useless. It then began to rise from a waste product to a luxury article. Countless varieties were made, and it was used in various ways. It was, for instance, like *garum*, mixed with old *mulsum* until it became sweet enough to be drunk. And it was served with oysters, sea-urchins, and innumerable other delicacies. Pliny mentions also its therapeutic qualities.

Apart from plain wine (*merum* or *vinum*), several wine preparations were used for cooking. It is generally known that cooking-wine has to be reduced in order to impart its full flavour to the dish. Nowadays we do this usually as part of the preparation of the dish in question. If, for instance, we make a sauce or gravy with wine we add the wine and let it boil fiercely until it is sufficiently reduced. The Roman cooks had this done beforehand, and used wine or must reduced to various degrees ready made. According to the degree of reduction, it was called *caroenum*, *defrutum* (or *defritum*), or *sapa*. The definitions given by various classical authors do not all agree with each other. According to Varro and Columella, *defrutum* is must reduced by boiling to one-third of its volume; according to Pliny, it should be reduced to half of its volume. Palladius gives the following definitions (XI, xviii):

Now about the preparation of *defrutum*, *caroenum*, and *sapa*. Although all three are made from the same substance, namely from must, the method of their preparation modifies both their names and their properties. For *defrutum* has its name from "boiling down," and it is ready when it is reduced to a thick consistency. *Caroenum* is ready when it has lost one-third of its volume with two-thirds remaining, *sapa*, when it has been reduced to one-third. The latter is improved when quinces are cooked with it and fig wood is added to the fire.

We usually made *defrutum* from tinned grape-juice—fresh must being unobtainable—which we reduced to one-third of its volume. It gives an excellent flavour to all kinds of sauces, and adds a very pleasant slight sweetness to the dish. We made our *caroenum* of white or red wine according to the dish it was used for, reducing the wine to two-thirds of its volume. Another specially prepared cooking-wine is the *passum*. Like *defrutum*, it was used to sweeten sauces. It is not only sweeter than *defrutum*, but has a different flavour. Palladius (XI, xix) even says that one can use it like honey. Columella gives two elaborate recipes for the preparation of *passum* (XII, 39):

Mago gives the following directions how to make the best *passum*, and I have made it myself like this. Gather early grapes when they are fully ripe, removing mouldy or damaged berries. Fix in the ground forks or stakes 4 feet apart to support reeds and join them together with poles. Then place the reeds on top and spread your grapes in the sun, covering them at night so that they do not get wet from the dew. Then, when they have dried, pick the berries off the stalks and put them in a cask or wine-jar and pour the best possible must over them so that the berries are completely covered. When saturated put them on the sixth day in a wicker basket and press them in the wine press and extract the *passum*. Next tread the grape-skins, having added freshest must which you have made from other grapes that were left to dry in the sun for three days. Mix together and put the whole mash through the wine-press, and this *passum* of the second pressing put immediately in vessels which you seal so that it does not become too rough. Then, after 20 or 30 days, when it has ceased fermenting, strain it into other vessels, seal their lids with gypsum immediately, and cover with skins.

If you wish to make *passum* from the "bee" grapes gather the whole grapes, clear away damaged berries, and throw them out. Then hang them up on poles. See to it that the poles are always in the sun. As soon as the berries are sufficiently shrivelled pick them off and put them without the stalks in a vessel and tread them well with your feet. When you have made one layer of them sprinkle old wine on and tread another layer of grapes over it and sprinkle this also with wine. Do the same with a third layer and, after having added wine, leave for five days. Then tread with your feet and press the grapes in a wicker basket. Some people prepare old rain-water for this, boiling it down to a third of its volume, and then, when they have made raisins in the manner described above, they take the boiled-down rain-water instead of wine, doing everything else in a manner similar to that described above. This process is very cheap where there is plenty of wood, and in use it is even sweeter than the *passum* described above.

Instead of *passum* we have used very sweet Spanish wine, being aware, of course, that this wine provides only the sweetness required, but not the original flavour.

Mulsum, wine mixed with honey, occurs in our recipes only on a few occasions. But as it is the drink that accompanied the first course of a Roman dinner it is of equal importance with the other wine preparations. Columella gives a recipe for its preparation (XII, 41):

Best *mulsum*. Make in the following way: take right from the vat must called *lixivum*, which is that which has come out from the grapes before they have been too much trodden, but make it with grapes from vines that grow winding around trees and that have been gathered on a dry day. Take 10 lb. of best honey to three gallons of must, mix thoroughly, and put it in a wine-jar which you seal with gypsum. Have it placed in a store-room. If you wish to make more add honey in the proportion indicated above. After 31 days the jar should be opened, and the must has to be strained into another vessel, which again is to be sealed and then placed in the smoke.

Pliny has other ideas about *mulsum*. He says (*Nat. Hist.* XXII, 24, 53 (113–114)) that it is always better to make *mulsum* from dry wine, since it mixes better with the honey, a complete mixture being impossible with sweet wine. The *mulsum* made from dry wine has other virtues besides—for instance, it does not cause flatulence. It whets the appetite for food. When drunk cold it relieves stomach-ache. It also makes you stout. Pliny proceeds to tell an anecdote about Pollio Romilius, who, asked by Augustus how he had managed to become a centenarian, answered, "By using *mulsum* for the inside and oil for the outside."

For our *mulsum* we used dry white wine. We did, however, not let the mixture stand for a month, but used it fresh. The proportion given by Columella works out at roughly 6 oz. of honey to a pint of wine, but we took about two tablespoonfuls to the ordinary bottle of wine. It is a very refreshing drink, an agreeable apéritif, and one can use very cheap wine, which in its pure form would hardly be drinkable.

In some of our recipes cheese is mentioned among the ingredients. There was a great variety of Roman cheeses. Apart from Vestine cheese, in the immediate neighbourhood of Rome—which occurs in our cookery-book—Pliny mentions (*Nat. Hist.* XI, 42, 97 (240–242)) cheeses from the region of Nîmes; from the Alps; from the Apennines; Sarsina cheese from Umbria; Luni cheese from the border district between Etruria and Liguria. This latter could weigh up to 1000 lb. Columella's cheese-making recipes give us an idea what Roman cheese must have been like (VII, viii). He mentions thin cheese that is to be sold as quickly as possible, as it does not keep. Hard cheese that keeps longer is made from fresh milk not mixed with water. It is curdled with rennet from lamb or kid, or with the flower of wild thistle (or artichoke), or seeds of saffron, or with the sap of fig-trees. But the best cheeses contain only very little of any of these things. The proportion of rennet to milk must be at least the weight of one silver denarius to the pail. The milk is to be kept at a certain temperature, but not put on the fire. As soon as it has thickened it is transferred into wicker baskets or moulds so that the whey can percolate. One may either let it drain away slowly or promote the draining by pressure. The cheese is then taken out of the baskets or moulds and put in a cool place on clean boards sprinkled with pounded salt. After hardening it is pressed again to make it quite compact. It is once more treated with salt and compressed with weights. Then it is set in rows on wicker-work trays to drain thoroughly. This cheese is suitable for export overseas.

Cheese to be eaten fresh is taken out of the baskets and dipped into salt and brine and then dried a little in the sun. Hand-pressed cheese is made by breaking up the slightly curdled milk, then pouring hot water over it and making the shapes by hand or in box-wood moulds. Columella also mentions smoked cheese, which is first hardened in brine and then coloured in the smoke of apple-tree wood.

Most of the sauces in our book are thickened with *amulum*. We have translated this word for the sake of convenience as 'cornflour,' for this is the starch most frequently used for this purpose to-day. The *amulum* was, however, wheat-starch. Pliny relates how it is manufactured (*Nat. Hist.* XVIII, 7, 17 (76)):

> Starch is made from every kind of wheat and fine wheat, but the best comes from three-month wheat. For its invention we are indebted to the island of Chios. And from there comes the variety most highly praised to-day. It takes its name from the fact that it is made without a mill. Next to that made of the three-month wheat comes that made of the lightest wheat. It is soaked in fresh water in wooden tubs so that the grain is covered, and the water changed five times a day. It is better if this is done also during the night, so that it gets mixed evenly. Before the softened grain goes sour it is strained through linen or through wicker baskets and poured on a tiled floor spread with leaven, and left so as to thicken in the sun. Next to starch from Chios that from Crete is most highly praised, then that from Egypt—it is tested by its smoothness, its light weight, and its freshness—and it has also been mentioned by Cato among ourselves.

Finally, at least a word must be said about the famous *silphium*, also called *laserpitium* and *laser*. Pliny has devoted a long chapter to this herb (XIX, 3, 15 ff. (38 ff.)). From him and Theophrastus (*Hist. plant.* VI, 3) we gain a great deal of information about it. The silphium grew in abundance in Cyrenaica, and was one of the chief exports of that province. It had become a kind of symbol of Cyrenaica, so that it appears on the coins of Cyrene, and even on reliefs. But in spite of all this no one has been able to identify the plant. In fact, it was already extinct in Cyrenaica in Pliny's time. He says that only a small quantity could be discovered under Nero, and this was sent to him. Otherwise it was only from Persia, Armenia, and Media that silphium was still imported, but this was of far inferior quality to that of Cyrenaica. The silphium from Cyrenaica was apparently expensive even when it was still grown in great quantities. Pliny mentions that under the consulate of C. Valerius and M. Herennius (93 B.C.) thirty pounds of silphium were sent to Rome and given to the State.

Although the identity of the Cyrenaican silphium cannot be established, that of the Persian variety is fairly certain: it was most probably the asafœtida, also called Devil's dung. This plant has retained its importance in the Middle East to this day, and it is used for pharmaceutical purposes also in the north.[12]

We know from Pliny that the juice of both the stem and the root was used. Its costliness is well illustrated by our recipe I, x: how to make an ounce of silphium last. The Cyrenaican variety is mentioned expressly only twice in our book; usually it simply prescribes 'laser.' Apicius himself may still have known and used the Cyrenaican silphium, but our late fourth- or early fifth-century compiler could only have known the Persian or Armenian varieties.

In recipes where *laser* is prescribed we have used asafœtida extract obtainable at chemists. It is very strong, and must be used with the utmost caution. The tiniest drop gives just enough flavour. If more than a minute quantity is taken the entire dish may be spoiled. But, used with care, it gives a delicious flavour, especially in combination with fish.

IV. ROMAN KITCHENS AND COOKING UTENSILS

by Joan Liversidge

The type of Roman kitchen about which we know most is well illustrated by the discoveries made during the excavations of Pompeii, where several of them which had obviously been in use at the time of the eruption of Vesuvius in A.D. 79 were found. Their most recognizable feature is the hearth, which consists of a raised platform of masonry faced on top with tiles, sometimes edged with a curb, and with a coating of *opus signinum* along the front. Arched openings in the front of the platform nearer the floor-level lead to fuel bins that are roughly constructed of rubble and tile.[13] Arrangements for providing water for cooking and washing-up are also sometimes found, as are the supports for the stone or wooden tables used for the preparation of food.[14]

Much of the cooking was done on small iron tripods and gridirons over burning charcoal. Pl. I shows in greater detail the hearth in the kitchen of the House of the Vettii at Pompeii, with cooking-vessels still standing on three-legged tripods, and a tripod and a gridiron found on Scottish sites appear on Pl. IIIa. Both of these can be paralleled from occupation sites in many parts of the Roman world, although the arrangement of the gridiron bars and cross-bars varies a little; and there does not seem to be much room for doubt that when Apicius refers to a *craticula* he means a grid-iron of this type.

Other fuel beside charcoal, however, must have been used, as Apicius refers to certain dishes being smoked. Possibly wood was also burnt on the raised hearth, the smoke escaping through

a vent in the kitchen wall, while the sausages or the sucking-pig
were hung on a well-placed hook over the fire. It is interesting
to remember that the kitchens in the House of the Dioscuri
may have been unroofed, apart from a canvas awning which
could be spread out in bad weather, and so a larger wood fire
lit on a brazier or some form of portable hearth would be a
possibility. One of the discoveries made at Pompeii was a
cooking-stove consisting of a low iron frame with a cement
hearth which could presumably have served for either wood or
charcoal. Four movable cross-bars are placed across the frame
at one end, and there are two rounded supports for pans.[15]
Some of the very ornamental water-heaters that were found
at Pompeii may have been used for reheating or keeping dishes
warm, or for cooking by the *bain-marie* process. One very
elaborate bronze heater is in the shape of a square battlemented
fortress with a tower at each corner covered by a hinged lid.
Water could be poured in through the top of the towers to
stand inside the hollow frame which formed the castle walls.
It could also be drawn off by a faucet in the centre of one side,
and was heated by a fire which was placed in an iron pan in
the centre.[16] Other heaters were cylinder-shaped, with the fire
at the bottom and a water container on top, usually covered by
a lid.[17] Large bronze bowls with flat rims have sometimes
been discovered in the rich Belgian barrow burials, usually
accompanied by smaller, shallower dishes which just fitted on
the top of the deep bowls. Their use is uncertain, but as they
show no signs of ever having been placed on a fire it has been
suggested that the large bowl was filled with hot water, and food
was placed in the shallower bowls to cook or be kept hot. This
would be an even closer approximation to the *bain-marie* process than the big heaters (Pl. II, No. 2).[18]

For such dishes as the sucking-pig suspended in a basket in
a cauldron of boiling water (VIII, vii, 4) these hearths and
braziers seem a little cramped, and perhaps in country kitchens
at least the older method of slinging the cauldron over a large
wood fire still prevailed, the smoke escaping through an aper-

ture in the roof. A clear picture of this appears on the side of a Roman altar found at Bonn.[19] It shows the iron chain hanging from a stout ring apparently fixed into the ceiling or a cross-beam, with a hook on the end with the cauldron handle looped over it. On the other side of the altar a servant is seen approaching carrying a pig on his back. Numerous cauldron chains of this type have been found in Roman and pre-Roman contexts in Britain and elsewhere.[20] Boars and other larger animals were also roasted on spits[21] over a wood fire, and Apicius himself refers to the smoke of the burning laurel and cypress branches when he is advising the careful housekeeper how to purify stale *liquamen* (I, vi). He also says, when cooking pork in recipe VII, x, "brown its fat on a glowing hot brazier," and here one can imagine the cook's assistant plying the bellows at a charcoal fire; but for *conditum paradoxum*, described in I, i, 1, as heated in a brass vessel over a fire of dry sticks, wood must have been employed, and from the quantities the brass vessel must have been a large one, which would hardly fit over the small tripods and gridirons.

The ovens used for baking and roasting were constructed of rubble and tiles, shaped like a low beehive, and provided with some kind of flue in front to provide a draught.[22] Wood or charcoal fires were lit inside them, the ashes were raked out as soon as the required temperature was reached, and the food was put in, the mouth of the oven being covered over to retain the heat. Small rectangular ovens working on the same principle were actually discovered standing on the hearth in the kitchens in the House of the Dioscuri at Pompeii. They may have been used for baking pastry, as a pastry mould was found near by. Some recipes, such as III, x, 2, for leeks cooked rolled in cabbage-leaves, or IV, ii, 4 or 33, for *patinae*, direct that the leeks or the pans containing the *patinae* are to be placed "among the coals" or "placed in the ashes" (*thermospodium*); such directions may refer to one of these ovens before all the ashes were removed, or they might mean among the ashes of a portable hearth. Then there was the *clibanus*, a small portable oven of earthenware, iron, bronze, or occasionally of more precious metals.[23]   This was also chiefly used to bake bread or cakes and keep dishes hot, as it could be placed on a table in the dining-room.   Apicius directs that the *clibanus* was to be used for roasting mutton in a frying-pan (VII, v, 5); while the stuffed dormice mentioned in VIII, ix, are either to be placed on a tile and cooked in the oven (*furnus*), or else put in the *clibanus*.   From literary sources we know that this form of small oven had a rounded vault wider at the base than at the top and double walls.   A charcoal fire must have been made under the inner floor, the heat percolated between the walls, and the fumes escaped through small holes in the outer covering.

In some of his recipes Apicius refers to the various kinds of cooking vessels to be used for various dishes.   With the possible exception of the frying-pan (*fretale* or *sartago*) none of them can be identified with absolute certainty, but the collections of kitchen equipment sometimes recovered from military sites and the various discoveries made at Pompeii enable us to suggest some strong probabilities.   One such hoard has been preserved from the Roman legionary fortress at Newstead, Scotland, and it can now be seen in the National Museum of Scottish Antiquities in Edinburgh.   It includes a gridiron and seven cooking-vessels of various shapes and sizes, all showing traces of burning and hard usage; several of them have been repaired with bronze patches soldered into place (Pl. IIIa).   At Pompeii a further selection of cooking-vessels was found *in situ* on the hearth in the kitchen of the House of the Vettii (Pl. I).   Possibly the Latin word *caccabus* (which is the word most frequently used by Apicius, and which must include pans of several different sizes and shapes) applies to cooking-vessels of these types.   They are widespread, and similar examples have been found at Gneisenau, Germany,[24] and in Pannonia.[25] Some of the Pompeian examples have lids attached to the handles by small chains to help pull them off when hot and to prevent them getting lost.

PLATE III

(a) BRONZE VESSELS AND IRON GRIDIRON FROM
NEWSTEAD; IRON TRIPOD FROM CARLINGSWARK
LOCH HOARD

By courtesy of the National Museum of Antiquities, Scotland

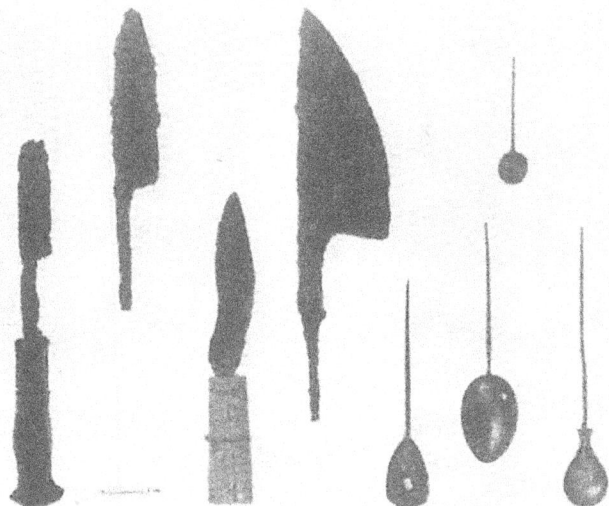

(b) BRONZE SPOONS AND IRON KNIVES, TWO WITH
ORIGINAL BONE HANDLES. BRAYBROOKE COLLECTION

By courtesy of Cambridge University Museum of Archæology and Ethnology
Photo L. P. Morley

PLATE IV

(a) TYPICAL ROMANO-BRITISH COOKING POTS

(b) (1) MORTARIUM. (2) BOWL PROBABLY USED
FOR COOKING

By courtesy of Cambridge University Museum of Archæology and Ethnology
Photos L. P. Morley

When Apicius tells the cook (*e.g.*, III, ii, 5; IV, ii, 22; VI, i, 3; or VI, ix, 13) to take a clean pan or a new pan he presumably means an earthenware cooking-pot, even when he still uses the word *patella*. Bronze pans would be too expensive to replace frequently, and they could also be got surprisingly clean with sea or desert sand. But sand is not such an efficient cleaning material for earthenware, and, with no soap available, these vessels, which were often made of very coarse pottery, must soon have become foul and unfit for service. They were also cheap to buy. Their shape and fabric varies at different places, as they were often made locally. Pl. IV*a* illustrates a few British examples.[26] In some cases Apicius is more explicit, and in VII, iv, 4, the Latin actually reads *patellam fictilem*, as opposed to *patellam aeneam* in IV, ii, 15. Elsewhere he uses the word for a pottery vessel, *cumana*, and this occurs in IV, ii, 11, as the casserole in which a *patina* of anchovies is cooked, or in VII, xiii, a recipe for an egg and milk sweet, to give only two examples. The *pultarius* used for cooking sauces or sea urchins may have been a small pottery or metal vessel.

For large joints, or for the soldiers' porridge, cauldrons of the type shown on the Bonn altar must have been needed. In VII, vii, 1, and VIII, vii, 11, the word *olla* is used for the vessel full of water in which the cook boils the sucking-pig or pig's stomach. In excavation reports *olla* is the term often used for the ordinary small cooking-pots. Here it must indicate something very much larger, more in the nature of a cauldron or a big camp kettle of the type sometimes found on military sites. One found at York bears a series of inscriptions telling us that first the century of Attilius Severus had it, and then it was passed on to the century of Aprilis—an interesting testimonial to the fact that these bronze vessels would be expected to remain in use for some time.[27] Other cauldrons have turned up on sites in Pannonia[28]; and, like the cauldron chains, several examples of Roman and pre-Roman cauldrons have been found in Britain.[29] The word *zema* which is used by Apicius in

3—R.C.B.

VIII, i, 10, and VIII, vi, 6, must also mean some kind of caul-dron.

The Roman frying-pan (*fretale* or *sartago*), of round or oval shape, and with a lip for pouring, is quite well known. Several bronze[30] examples have been found in Pompeii, and Pl. II, No. 5, illustrates a frying-pan now in the British Museum. Iron frying-pans were also used, and fragments of one discovered in London show that it had a movable handle which folded up when not in use.[31] Similar pans of a more oblong shape, and with folding handles with incised decoration and holes for suspension when not in use, are among a collection of Coptic cooking equipment found in Egypt, and now in the Royal Ontario Museum.[32] From the same collections come rect-angular iron trays with handles, and also a lip at each corner, designed for roasting or frying.[33] Possibly the *angularis* mentioned by Apicius in VII, iv, 1, was a vessel of this type, but it must have been deeper to allow for the layers of meat and oil-cake.

In Book IV Apicius refers frequently to pans he calls *patellae* and *patinae*, and here our evidence becomes very inconclusive. The *patella* is usually identified as a round, shallow pan with a handle, little deeper than a frying-pan[34]; it could appear at table as well as in the kitchen, and may have been the secular form of the *patera* used for religious purposes. A possible example of it is illustrated by Pl. II, No. 1. From the recipes, with their description of dishes built up with layers of oil cake, the *patina* must have been a deeper vessel. One authority describes it as a large, open pan of oblong form, and we wonder if certain oval or round bronze vessels usually lifted by a handle on each side or else provided with a long handle thicker than that of a frying-pan were not also *patinae*. One two-handled example was found at Pompeii,[35] another vessel which originally probably had a long handle has been noted from Carnuntum,[36] and the example illustrated (Pl. II, No. 3) comes from the Towneley Collection in the British Museum. The flat pottery bowls often found on Roman sites may also have been used for this purpose; they are rather like a round pie-dish, and the traces of soot occasionally found beneath their rims prove that they were used for cooking (Pl. IV, No. 2). Reference has already been made above to an earthenware *patella*, presumably a shallower bowl of this type.

Equipment for preparing and dishing up food resembles the implements in use for similar purposes to-day. Knives of all sizes are frequently found, usually made of iron, with bronze, wood, or bone handles (Pl. III*b*). Many examples of spoons are also known, made of bone, bronze, or silver, with round or oval bowls. The *cocleare* was a small spoon supposed to be used for eating eggs, and with a pointed handle convenient for picking snails or shellfish out of their shells. Larger spoons of bronze or iron, ladles and dippers (*trullae* and *simpula*), and meat-hooks were other items used in kitchen or dining-room. The strainers (*colae*) which are often mentioned in the recipes are a greater problem, as the long-handled bronze strainers with holes arranged in ornamental patterns are usually associated with the more decorative bronze vessels used for serving wine. Excavations have produced pottery bowls with holes in the bottom which could have been used as colanders,[37] and some liquids perhaps may have been strained through jelly-bags of muslin or some other similar textile. But when the contents of one pan have to be strained into another, and elaborate cooking operations are in progress, it seems that some of the plainer versions of the bronze strainers must have been used. Probably the small strainers of the type illustrated (Pl. II, No. 6), with their larger holes, belong in the kitchen. Many recipes begin by taking pepper or various herbs, which are put in the mortar and pounded or ground. While stone mortars may have been employed in some cases, the stout pottery bowls known to archæologists as *mortaria* probably did duty in most cases, and these are made with a sprinkling of grit baked into the fabric to help with the grinding process (Pl. IV*b*., No. 1). Stone or wooden pestles were used with them. Among the Coptic kitchen utensils in the Royal

Ontario Museum is a crescent-shaped iron blade with two rings for a wooden handle fixed in its back. This is believed to have been used for mincing meat.[38]

When the food was dished up it was placed on a *discus*—a word which is a general term for all kinds of dishes and plates of circular shape. Large platters and shallow bowls of silver, bronze, or pewter are frequently found in hoards of metal vessels, often decorated with incised patterns or designs in relief. The silver dishes in the Hildesheim treasure are among the most famous examples,[39] as are the numerous bronze bowls found at Pompeii. Fine pottery, particularly the red Samian-ware bowls, with their relief decoration, or the undecorated platters, must also have appeared in the dining-room. One of the more puzzling references made by Apicius is to something he calls a *conchiclar*, a vessel associated with certain dishes in Book V, iv. This may have been some kind of pan, but the existence at Pompeii of some very attractive bronze dishes fluted to resemble a scallop-shell suggests that the name *conchiclar* might refer to a dish of this shape in which the food was served, rather than to the saucepan in which it was cooked.[40] Larger dishes of the same kind could have been used as moulds. In IX, xiii, 1, a recipe for salt fish without fish, Apicius says that the mixture of liver and spices may be made into the shape of a fish or put in a mould if liked, and small moulds in the shape of a pig, a dressed hare, or a ham have actually been found at Pompeii.[41]

[1] W. Koehler, *Die Schule von Tours* (Berlin, 1930–33), Vol. I (text), pp. 288 f., 409. Pls. 114 *d–f.*

[2] Described in De Ricci and Wilson's *Census of the Medieval and Renaissance MSS. in the United States and Canada*, Vol. II, 1937, pp. 1310–1311.

[3] For the history of the two manuscripts in the Renaissance and the Apicius manuscript-tradition in general, see A. Campana, "Contributi alla biblioteca del Poliziano, IV. L'Apicio del Poliziano," *Il Poliziano e il suo tempo, Atti del IV convegno internazionale di*

studi sul Rinascimento (1954), Florence, 1957, pp. 198 ff., esp.
pp. 211 ff., where also previous literature on the subject is cited.
4 The following note on the *editio princeps* is contributed by Dr V.
Scholderer.
5 E. Brandt, *Untersuchungen zum Römischen Kochbuch* (Philologus,
Supplementband XIX, Heft III), Leipzig, 1927.
6 "Studien zu dem römischen Kochbuche des Apicius," *Sitzungs-
berichte der Bayer. Akad. der Wissenschaften*, 1920, 6. Abh.
7 On this sauce, see below, p. 21.
8 Translation by B. Flower.
9 See below, p. 25.
10 *Corpus Inscriptionum Latinarum* IV, 7110: "liquamen/optimum/
saccatum/Ex officina Umbrici Agathopi." I owe the reference
to the kindness of Miss J. Reynolds.
11 See below, p. 23.
12 See V. Vikentiev, "Le Silphium et le rite du renouvellement de
la vigeur," *Bull. de l'Institut d'Egypte*, XXXVII, 1 (1954–55),
p. 123 ff.
13 L. Richardson, "Pompeii: the Casa Dioscuri and its Painters,"
Memoirs of the American Academy in Rome (1955), p. 71.
14 J. Liversidge, "Kitchens in Roman Britain," *Archaeological
News Letter*, Vol. VI, No. 4 (1957) p. 83.
15 Tarbell, *Catalogue of Bronzes etc. in the Field Museum of Natural
History, Chicago* (reproduced from originals in the National
Museum of Naples), Field Museum of Natural History,
Chicago, No. 130, Vol. VII, No. 3 (1909), Fig. 105, p. 118.
16 *Ibid*, p. 117, Fig. 104.
17 *Ibid*, p. 116, Figs. 99, 100.
18 *Antiquité Classique* XXI (1952), p. 42, Fig. 2, No. 7; p. 57.
19 Espérandieu, *Bas-reliefs de la Gaule romaine*, XI (1938), No. 7762.
20 *Proceedings of the Society of Antiquaries of Scotland* LXXXVII
(1952–53), pp. 12 ff., 24, 26.
21 Virgil, *Æneid* I, 211; V, 102, 103.
22 Mau-Kelsey, *Pompeii: its Life and Art* (1902), p. 391.
23 Daremberg and Saglio, *Dictionnaire des Antiquités grecques et
romaines* I, ii (1887), Fig. 1633, p. 1246.
24 *Bericht d. Röm.-Germ. Kommission* (1912), p. 157, Fig. 76.
25 Radnoti, *Die Römischen Bronzegefässe von Pannonien* (1938),
Pls. XXXII, XXXIII.

38   THE ROMAN COOKERY BOOK

²⁶ The examples illustrated are all in the Cambridge University Museum of Archæology and Ethnology. See also *Antiquaries Journal* XXXI (1951), p. 154 ff., especially p. 156, No. 10, and p. 158, No. 21. I am indebted to Mr B. R. Hartley, M.A., for this reference.
²⁷ *Yorkshire Philosophical Society Annual Reports* (1935), p. 5; *Antiquaries Journal* XV, p. 198, Pl. 36.
²⁸ Radnoti, *op. cit.* (above, note 25), Pl. XXXVI, No. 3.
²⁹ *Proceedings of the Society of Antiquaries of Scotland* (above, note 20), p. 30.
³⁰ From the Towneley Collection. We are indebted to the Trustees of the British Museum for information about this vessel and the vessels illustrated by Pl. II.
³¹ London Museum Catalogue, No. 3, *London in Roman Times* (1930), p. 118, Fig. 41.
³² *American Journal of Archæology* XXV (1921), p. 44, Fig. 5.
³³ *Ibid.*, p. 47, Figs. 8, 9.
³⁴ Daremberg and Saglio, *op. cit.* (above, note 23), III, ii, p. 1301 under LOPAS.
³⁵ Mau-Kelsey, *op. cit.* (above, note 22), Fig. 204 r.
³⁶ Radnoti, *op. cit.* (above, note 25), Pl. XXXVI, No. 2.
³⁷ T. May, *Pottery found at Silchester* (1916), Pl. L, No. 70.
³⁸ *American Journal of Archæology* (above, note 32), p. 51, Fig. 12.
³⁹ Pernice and Winter, *Der Hildesheimer Silberfund* (1901).
⁴⁰ Tarbell, *op. cit.* (above, note 15), p. 132, Fig. 203.
⁴¹ Tarbell, *op. cit.* (above, note 15), p. 135, Figs. 224–226.

UNTRANSLATED TERMS

allec: see Introduction, p. 23.
caroenum: wine reduced by boiling, see Introduction, p. 23.
defrutum: must reduced by boiling, see Introduction, p. 23.
garum = *liquamen, q.v.*
hydrogarum: liquamen mixed with water, see Introduction, p. 23.
liquamen: see Introduction, p. 21.
mulsum: see Introduction, p. 25.
oenogarum: liquamen mixed with wine, see Introduction, p. 23.
oxygarum: liquamen mixed with vinegar, see Introduction, p. 23.
passum: see Introduction, p. 24.

MEASURES AND WEIGHTS

acetabulum = $\frac{1}{4}$ gill ($\frac{1}{8}$ pint).
calix = a wineglass-full.
cocleare = $\frac{1}{2}$ *cheme* (about a teaspoon).
cyathus = $\frac{1}{12}$ pint (either untranslated or given in pints).
drachma = $\frac{1}{8}$ oz. (translated: a handful).
hemina = $\frac{1}{2}$ pint.
ligula = spoonful (tablespoon).
quartarius = 1 gill ($\frac{1}{4}$ pint).
scrupulus = 1 scruple ($\frac{1}{24}$ oz.).
sextarius = 1 pint.
uncia = 1 oz.

ABBREVIATIONS

add. = added (by).
Br., Brandt = E. Brandt (*the page numbers refer to the book quoted on p. 12 of the Introduction*).
codd. = consensus of the manuscript tradition.
corr. = corrected (by).
del. = deleted (by).
E = MS. New York, Library of the Academy of Medicine, formerly Cheltenham, Phillipps Collection 275.
F. = B. Flower.
Giarratano = C. Giarratano, in Teubner edition of Apicius.
Guégan = B. Guégan, *Les Dix Livres de Cuisine d'Apicius* (Paris, 1933).
Humelberg = Apicius edition of G. Humelberg (Zürich, 1542).
R. = E. Rosenbaum.
rest. = original text of manuscripts restored (by).
Schuch = Apicius edition of T. Schuch (Heidelberg, 1874).
Teubner = Apicius edition of C. Giarratano and F. Vollmer (Leipzig, Teubner, 1922).
V = MS. Rome, Vatican Library (*Urb. lat.* 1146).
Vehling = J. D. Vehling, *Apicius: Cooking and Dining in Imperial Rome* (Chicago, 1936).
Vollmer = F. Vollmer, in Teubner edition of Apicius.
† = text corrupt.
[ ] = words or passages believed to be interpolations or errors

in the text, or considered to be glosses. If no footnotes are added these parentheses are already in the Teubner edition. These words or passages are as a rule not translated.

⟨ ⟩= in the Latin text: words or passages added by the present or previous editors. If not stated otherwise in footnotes these additions are already in the Teubner edition.

= in the English text: either corresponding to the Latin text; or words added by the translators for the sake of clarity.

EPIMELES

I. conditum paradoxum. II. conditum melizomum.
III. absinthium Romanum. IV. rosatum et violatium. V. oleum Liburnicum sic facies. VI. vinum ex
atro candidum facies. VII. de liquamine. VIII. ut
carnes sine sale quovis tempore recentes sint. IX. cal-
lum porcinum vel bubulum et unguellae coctae ut diu
durent. X. ut carnem salsam dulcem facias. XI. pis-
ces fricti ut diu durent. XII. ostrea ut diu durent.
XIII. ut uncia laseris toto tempore uti possis. XIV. ut
dulcia de melle diu durent. XV. ut mel malum bonum
facias. XVI. mel corruptum ut probes. XVII. uvae
ut diu serventur. XVIII. ut mala et mala granata diu
durent. XIX. ut mala Cydonia diu serventur. XX.
ficum recentem mala pruna pira cerasia ut diu serves.
XXI. citria ut diu durent. XXII. mora ut diu durent.
XXIII. holera ut diu serventur. XXIV. rapae ut diu
serventur. XXV. tubera ut diu serventur. XXVI.
duracina Persica ut diu serventur. XXVII. sales condi-
tos ad multa. XXVIII. olivas virides servare ut quovis
tempore oleum facias. XXIX. cuminatum in ostrea et
conchyliis. XXX. laseratum. XXXI. oenogarum in
tubera. XXXII. oxyporum. XXXIII. hypotrimma.
XXXIV. oxygarum digestibile. XXXV. moretaria.

BOOK I

THE CAREFUL HOUSEKEEPER

I. Spiced wine surprise. II. Spiced honey wine.
III. Roman vermouth. IV. Rose wine and violet
wine. V. Liburnian oil. VI. To make white wine out
of red wine. VII. On *liquamen*. VIII. How to keep
meat fresh as long as you like without pickling. IX.
How to keep pork or beef skin and cooked trotters.
X. To make salt meat sweet. XI. To preserve fried
fish. XII. To preserve oysters. XIII. How to make
one ounce of silphium last indefinitely. XIV. How to
preserve cakes made of honey. XV. How to make bad
honey good. XVI. How to find out if honey has gone
bad. XVII. To keep grapes fresh. XVIII. To keep
apples and pomegranates fresh. XIX. To keep quinces
fresh. XX. How to preserve fresh figs and apples,
plums, pears, and cherries. XXI. To preserve citron.
XXII. To preserve blackberries. XXIII. To preserve
green vegetables. XXIV. To preserve turnips. XXV.
To preserve truffles. XXVI. To preserve peaches.
XXVII. Aromatic salts to be used for many things.
XXVIII. To preserve green olives so as to make oil
at any time you wish. XXIX. Cumin sauce for oysters
and shell-fish. XXX. Silphium sauce. XXXI.
Oenogarum for truffles. XXXII. *Oxyporum.*
XXXIII. *Hypotrimma.* XXXIV. *Oxygarum*, to pro-
mote the digestion. XXXV. *Moretaria.*

I. Spiced wine surprise

1. Spiced wine surprise is made as follows. 15 lb. of
honey are put in a metal vessel into which you have previously
put 2 pints of wine, so as to boil down the wine while cooking
the honey. It is heated over a slow fire of dry wood, stirring
all the while with a stick; when it begins to boil over it is

43

I. CONDITUM PARADOXUM

1. CONDITI PARADOXI COMPOSITIO: mellis pondo XV in
aeneum vas mittuntur, praemissis vini sextariis duobus, ut in
coctura mellis vinum decoquas. quod igni lento et aridis lignis
calefactum, commotum ferula dum coquitur, si effervere
coeperit, vini rore compescitur, praeter quod subtracto igni in
se redit. cum perfrixerit, rursus accenditur. hoc secundo ac
tertio fiet, ac tum demum remotum a foco postridie despumatur.
tum ⟨mittis⟩ piperis uncias IV, iam triti masticis scripulos III,
folii et croci dragmas singulas, dactylorum ossibus torridis
quinque, isdemque dactylis vino mollitis, intercedente prius
suffusione vini de suo modo ac numero, ut tritura lenis habeatur.
his omnibus paratis supermittis vini lenis sextarios XVIII.
carbones perfecto aderunt † duo milia.[1]   (1)

2. CONDITUM MELIZOMUM VIATORIUM. Conditum melizomum perpetuum, quod subministratur per viam peregrinanti:
piper tritum cum melle despumato in cupellam mittis conditi
loco, et ad momentum quantum sit bibendum, tantum aut
mellis proferas aut vini misceas. sed suaserit[2] nonnihil vini
melizomo mittas, adiciendum propter mellis exitum solutiorem.

(2)

II. APSINTHIUM ROMANUM

APSINTHIUM ROMANUM SIC FACIES: conditi Camerini praecep-
tis utique pro apsinthio cessante: in cuius vicem absenti Pontici
purgati terendique unciam, Thebaicam dabis, masticis, folii,
costi scripulos senos, croci scripulos III, vini eiusmodi sextarios
XVIII. carbones amaritudo non exigit.[3]   (3)

---

[1] *duo milia* codd., obelized by Br. (p. 24 f.) who thinks it might be
a wrong translation from the Greek.
[2] *suaserit* codd., rest. by Br.
[3] Br. (p. 23 f.) rest. reading of codd., eliminating only *III* after
folii.

checked by adding ⟨cold⟩ wine; it also sinks when removed from the fire. When cool it is heated once more. This must be done a second and third time, and only then is it removed from the fire, and skimmed on the following day. Then take 4 oz. pepper, 3 scruples of pounded mastic, a handful each of aromatic leaf[1] and saffron, 5 roasted date-stones, the dates softened in wine, having previously been soaked in wine of the right kind and quality, so as to produce a soft mash. These preparations completed, pour over 18 pints of sweet wine. In the end add coals, if it is too bitter.[2]

2. SPICED HONEY-WINE FOR TRAVELLERS. Spiced honey wine which keeps for ever is given to people on a journey. Put pounded pepper with skimmed honey in a small vat just as for spiced wine and, when required for drinking, mix part of the honey with some wine. It is advisable to add a little wine to the honey-mixture in order to make the honey run out more freely.

II. ROMAN VERMOUTH

ROMAN VERMOUTH prepare as follows. According to the recipes for Camerinian spiced wine, if you do not have any vermouth: in its stead take 1 oz. cleaned and pounded Pontian vermouth, 1 date, 6 scruples each of mastic, aromatic leaves,[3] and costmary, 3 scruples of saffron, 18 pints of the proper kind of wine. As it should be bitter, you need not add coal.

----

[1] See note (1) to I, xv, 1.
[2] The translation follows Brandt's suggestion; see note to the Latin text. Cp. also the recipe for Roman vermouth, below.
[3] See note (1) to I, xv, 1.

III. ⟨ROSATUM ET VIOLATIUM⟩

1. ROSATUM SIC FACIES: folia rosarum, albo sublato, lino inseris et sutilis facias, et vino quam plurimas infundes, ut septem diebus in vino sint. post septem dies rosam de vino tollis, et alias sutiles recentes similiter mittis, ut per dies septem in vino requiescant, et rosam eximis. similiter et tertio facies, et rosam eximis, et vinum colas, et, cum ad bibendum voles uti, addito melle rosatum conficies. sane custodito ut rosam a rore siccam et optimam mittas. Similiter, ut supra, et de ⟨viola⟩ violatium facies, et eodem modo melle temperabis.

(4)

2. ROSATUM SINE ROSA SIC FACIES: folia citri viridia in sportella palmea in dolium musti mittes antequam ferveat, et post quadraginta dies exime. cum necesse fuerit, mel addes et pro rosato utere.

IV

OLEUM LIBURNICUM SIC FACIES: in oleo Hispano mittes helenium et cyperi et folia lauri non vetusta, tunsa omnia et cribellata, ad levissimum pulverem redacta, et sales frictos et tritos, et per triduum vel plus permisce diligenter. post haec aliquanto tempore patere requiescere, et Liburnicum omnes putabunt.   *(5)*

V

VINUM EX ATRO CANDIDUM FACIES: lomentum ex faba factum vel ovorum trium alborem in lagonam mittis et diutissime agitas: alia die erit candidum. et cineres vitis albae idem faciunt.

(6)

III. ⟨ROSE WINE AND VIOLET WINE⟩

1. ROSE WINE. Rose wine you will make like this: Thread together rose-leaves from which the white part has been removed, and steep as many as possible in wine for seven days. After seven days take the rose-leaves out of the wine, and in the same way put in other fresh rose-leaves threaded together, to rest seven days in the wine, then take them out. Repeat a third time, take out the rose-leaves, strain the wine, and, when you want to use it for drinking, add honey to make rose wine. But take care to use the best rose-leaves, when the dew has dried off them. Make violet wine in the same way as above, and mix with honey in the same way.

2. ROSE WINE WITHOUT ROSE-LEAVES. Put fresh citron-leaves[1] in a basket made of palm-leaves, into a jar of must before it ferments, and take out after 40 days. When required, add honey and use as rose wine.

IV

LIBURNIAN OIL make as follows. To Spanish oil add helenium[2] and cyperus-root and fresh bay-leaves, all this pounded and sifted until reduced to very fine powder, and dried and pounded salt. Mix these ingredients for three days or longer. After this allow the mixture to rest for some time, and everybody will believe it is Liburnian oil.

V

TO MAKE WHITE WINE OUT OF RED WINE. Put bean-meal or three egg-whites into the flask and stir for a very long time. The next day the wine will be white. The white ashes of vine have the same effect.

[1] See note to I, xii, 5.
[2] calamint?

www.ingramcontent.com/pod-product-compliance
Lightning Source LLC
Chambersburg PA
CBHW051049030426
42339CB00006B/261